DRAW ME 387 BAKED BEANS IN 10 SECONDS...

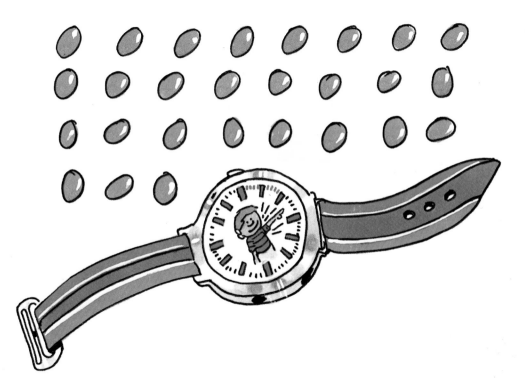

and other PUZZLES by BILL TIDY

Andersen Press · London

To all Children Like Me

Copyright © 1991 by Bill Tidy

The rights of Bill Tidy to be identified as the author and illustrator of this work have been asserted by him in
accordance with the Copyright, Designs and Patents Act, 1988.

First published in 1991 by Andersen Press Ltd., 20 Vauxhall Bridge Road, London SW1V 2SA.
Published in Australia by Random Century Australia Pty., Ltd., 20 Alfred Street, Milsons Point, Sydney,
NSW 1061. All rights reserved. Colour separated in Switzerland by Photolitho AG, Gossau, Zürich.
Printed and bound in Italy by Grafiche AZ, Verona.
10 9 8 7 6 5 4 3 2 1
British Library Cataloguing in Publication Data available.
ISBN 0 86264 347 3

Hello!
This is a drawing book with a difference! I'm going to ask you to draw things in 10 seconds which will seem absolutely impossible and stupid but you can do it easily if you,

THINK!

I'll show you how it's done by starting with an easy one ... the name of this book!

READY!

Oh, by the way, do all of your drawings in pencil so that they can be rubbed out and then your friends can have a go!

Right! Say I asked you to draw 387 baked beans in 10 seconds starting now... What would you do?

Well, anyone who started drawing beans one by one is going to take years and you have got only 10 seconds.

To solve the problems in the book you have to do one thing.

THiMK? NO!

THiLK? NO!

THINK! YES!

You've got it!
You have to think!
Now where would that
many beans be? On a plate?
Yes, but you could see them
all on a plate and you'd have
to draw them all. Where else – Ha!

All you do is draw a can of baked beans. Simple isn't it?

Great, we can get started. Take your pencil and start up brain.

1 Draw me 160,000 cubic litres of hot air, 2,000 metres of silk, 40 metres of rope and a basket.

2 Draw me 429 white grapes, 2 cups of water and some sugar.

3 Draw me the 36 photos Charlie Smith took on his holiday last year.

I'LL GO DOWN TO THE CELLAR FOR IT!

DELAYS
MAJORCA 14 HOURS
ALICANTE 16 HOURS
RIMINI 14 HOURS

VOTE FOR ME

THERE'S ANOTHER 5000 CUBIC LITRES OF HOT AIR!

WE SHOULD'VE GONE BY 160,000 CUBIC LITRES OF HOT AIR...

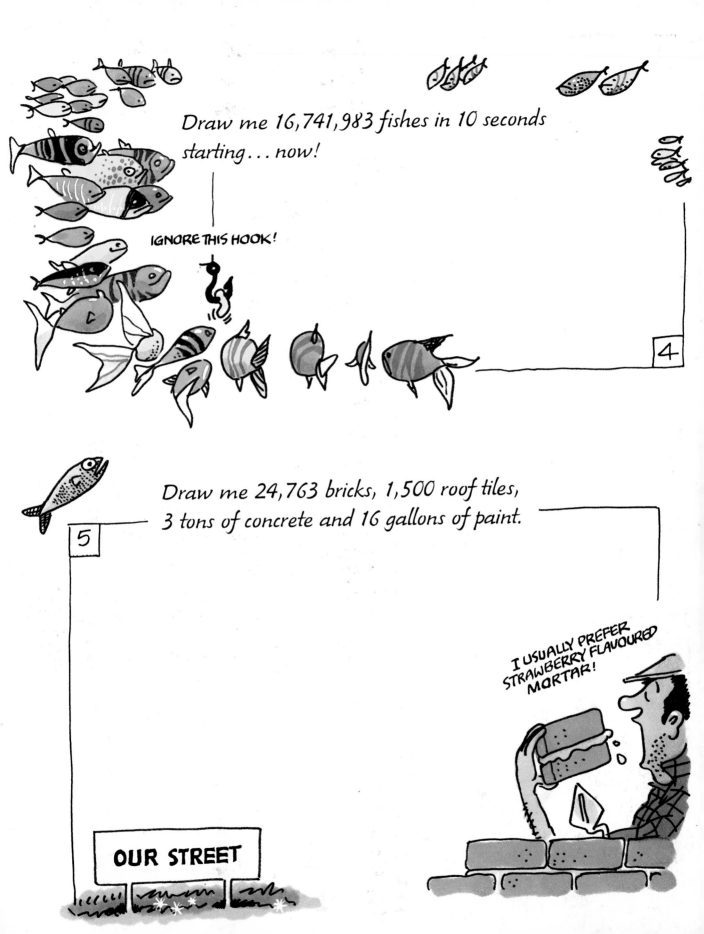

Draw me 944 hamburgers, no mustard, no buns.

I DON'T THINK I'D LIKE TO TAKE ON 944 CHEESEBURGERS!

13

Draw me the team which came after the 'A' team.

14

TEAM

Draw me 363 fleas ... and no scratching till you've finished!

15

I SAID 'NO SCRATCHING!'

Draw me 2 pints of sour milk and 69,947,382,508,694 friendly bacteria.

16

↑
UNFRIENDLY BACTERIA.

Draw me at least 928,483,617,428 bubbles.

17

Draw me 426 people eating a meal, watching a film and going to Disneyland at 540 miles per hour.

HUH, I SAW THIS FILM LAST TIME AT 553 MPH!

18

Draw me 426 apples ...

19

... and draw me 661,409,903,721 million tons of rock with some snow on the top.

20

YOU'LL BE SICK EATING ALL THOSE APPLES AND THAT ROCK WONT DO YOUR TEETH ANY GOOD!

Draw me 14 woolly jerseys (large),
16 woolly scarves (long),
9 pairs of grey socks and
11 pairs of grey gloves.

TO SIDNEY
FROM
MARY HADDA

21

Draw me
620,000,000 barrels
of crude oil a day.

22

...and draw me
149,881,622 bees...

THIS WAY THEY
DON'T RECOGNISE
ME!

23

...and 429,897,605,437 ants!

NO NEED TO
BE CRUDE!

THIS WAY THEY
DO RECOGNISE
ME!

24

CRUMBS!

That's just what I was going to say!
Draw me 192,476 bread crumbs.

I KNOW THIS ONE!

25

26

... and
27,000
windows...

... and finally in
this section...

FINISH

27

Draw me... in 10 seconds...
6 T-shirts,
3 pairs of trousers,
3 pairs of shorts,
2 pairs of swimming trunks,
3 shirts,
8 pairs of socks,
2 sets of underwear,
towel,
2 pairs of trainers,
toilet bag,
suntan oil
and a book.

MY ARM'S A BIT TIRED!

SO'S MINE!

How are you doing so far? It's easy isn't it, but things are no fun if they're easy all of the time, so let's move on to Famous People puzzles. These are a bit harder, but, in each one there's a clue to help you decide what to draw. Here's an example.

Famous People

Draw me Sir Henry Flimpton (1704-1791) inventor of the famous Flimpton sack. HF as he was always known designed a sack open at both ends to make it easier to empty. This information won't help you to solve the riddle but at least it will stop you doing anything as stupid and it may help if I tell you he is buried in St Gumps Churchyard.

Local dimwits testing the sack not far from where HF was buried.

Did you get it?
Sir Henry Flimpton if he lived 200 years ago must be dead and you don't know what he looks like so the clue is 'he is buried in St Gumps Churchyard' and your drawing should look like this:

R.I.P
HF

Right, let's go!
Draw me Paddy St Murphy,
the famous snail trainer
and eater of ladies
bicycles, whose last wish
was to be buried under
the first set of traffic
lights erected in Paris
in 1920.

STOP!

Draw me the very distinctive
autograph of Herr Richter, inventor of the Richter
Scale, a way of measuring the shakiness of earthquakes.

Draw me Tarzan's brother Ted,
who was the first man to swim the mighty
River Zimboco underwater, with a bird on his head.

TED!

Draw me Amanda Bollington Scrowde and her husband Nigel before and after they went over
Niagara Falls, together,
in a barrel on Friday
12 February 1944.

ARE'NT THEY TUBBY!

Draw me
the Great Pharaoh Khufu when last seen with all his possessions.
These included his sword, shield, spear, helmet, underpants, slippers,
bed, potty, 'jamas, boat, false nose, towel and toothbrush.
You've got ten seconds to do it!

IT TOOK YOU 10 SECONDS.
IT'S TAKEN ME MORE
THAN 3000 YEARS!

Draw me 'Exploding Boots' Frummel just after he had eaten a Dynamite and pickle sandwich...

33

...and the attempt by Signor Umberto Umbrello, the world's strongest man, to pull with his teeth a 290 ton locomotive and 18 goods wagons carrying 1,000 bags of cement, across the frozen River Blobsk, at just about the time of the rapid summer thaw. He didn't use the bridge.

YOU'VE MISSED IT BUT THERE'LL BE ANOTHER ONE IN ABOUT A YEAR!

34

Draw me Stanley 'Sconehead' Wisbeech, who claimed at the 1977 World Headache Exhibition in Tokyo, that if a huge 2,500 ton block of concrete was dropped on his head, he would suffer no harm whatsoever!

Draw me 109 years old Lee How Pong, designer of the 'Elderly Dragon' Swamp and Quicksand Walking Frame for old age pensioners. Watched by some hopeful users, he demonstrates for the first time the new 'speedo model' for over 90 year olds on the treacherous Wing Hee Swamp!

Draw me Ireland's bravest soldier Tamara Przwckzc, who was so tough and fit, that she could jump over a wall. She was afraid of nothing except mice.

Draw me Mervyn 'The Axe' Pronk, Canada's fastest tree feller, beating every other lumberjack by more than three trees in the 1985 championship.

38

39 Draw me the massive 4,500,000 ton iceberg, which after striking the liner Titanic, was caught by a freak wind and carried to Africa.

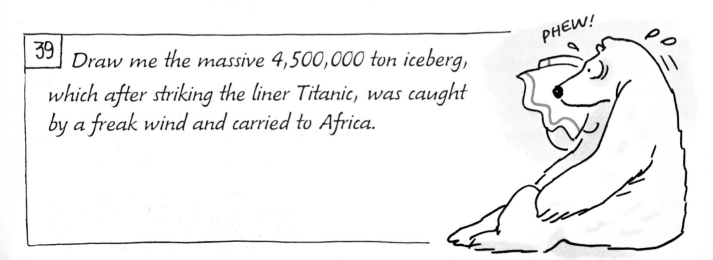

Draw me the result of the attempt by the Flying Frenellis to swap trapezes high above the streets of Tokyo, while blindfolded, wearing boxing gloves and each carrying a box of frozen squid. Ron, Don, John, Lon, Bron and Con came from the left and Nita, Rita, Pepita, Concita, Juanita, Melita, Rosita and Carmencita came from the right.

THAT REMINDED ME OF THE WORLD HEADACHE CHAMPIONSHIPS!

Draw me musical maestro, Eduardo Squampolino, the first man to discover that a high note played on a trumpet could cause an avalanche.

TRUMPET & SPADE MUSIC

And now for the most spectacular and hardest 'Draw Me' in the book…

Draw me 126 elephants, 27 London double-decker buses, 9 Boeing 747 jumbo jets and the largest tanker ever built, the 999,000 tons Oiliver Slick!

Time's up. Any luck? I know it's very difficult but there's one person who might help you. H.P. Stromboli, the greatest illusionist of all time, used every one of the 'Draw me' elephants, buses, jumbo jets and ships in his 1984 Las Vegas stage act... You've got another 10 seconds...

Criminals

We'll move now to people who became famous for the wrong reason. Criminals! Draw me the disguises used by these famous nasties!

43

William 'No Beard' Guskitt

44

'One Leg' Wibley

45

Geraldine '29 Fingers' Twitherton

46

Harry 'The Monk' Stibbins

47
Thomas 'Canary' Bulstrode

48

49
Ivor 'Handstand' Le Spit

Shortie 'O' Fogworth

Draw me the world famous oil painting by Van Scrumphausen of Emperor Wan Hu Chi, his 941 wives and 2,614 children all playing in front of the incredible 3,000 room Golden Palace of Fung Ho.

50

The picture, worth £384,000,000 was in the Louvre Museum in Paris until yesterday when it was cut from its frame and stolen by a man eating a choc-ice. It has not been recovered.

Draw me the famous escape attempt by F.P. Nilly, Mad Trousers
Frampton, the Skonk Triplets and High Wire Haggerty
when they made their unsuccessful try to be the first men
to exit from Dartmoor Prison
by tightrope from their top floor cell
to the wall.

The Wonders of Nature...

Let's look at the wonders of nature...
Draw me the most difficult of all
reptiles to see, the three-spotted
rock lizard, resting on a
rock in Rock Valley.

ROCK VALLEY

Draw me a flock of
336 Snelby ducks,
the shyest of all
creatures, which will
only fly in cloud.

54

Draw me 2 polar bears
playing on an iceberg.

53

I CAN SEE YOU!

Draw me the huge herd of over 2,000,000 wilderbeste, which emigrate south every year from the grassy plains of N'Konko N'Konko in N'Konko to the grassy plains of M'bonko M'bonko in M'bonko, unless it's raining.

55

56

Draw me Colonel Aubrey Melchett-Boakes and his friend Lady Harriet String the great explorers, who were unfortunately swallowed by a giant Amazonian snake.

Sport

Interested in sport? Even if you're not try these!
Draw me the 1972 final of the World Tug of War Championships
in Moscow when the incredible Bologna Big Bellies...

57

58

Draw me the beautiful, flame-haired Lynda
Pottleton-Snitterby and her black mare,
Jockey Holleysticks the III, when she almost
completed a clear round at the 1972
Castle Thrumpton horse trials.

THE
WATER
JUMP

... met the legendary San Francisco Hamburger, Tomato-sauce, Pickle and Relish Stuffers. They were the heaviest teams ever to reach the final but no prize was awarded on this occasion.

Well, that's it. (Apart from: Draw me 9 hippoptami asleep in a pool with just one awake.)

WHEN THEY GO TO SLEEP I'VE GOT NOBODY TO STAND ON!

I suppose you got most of them. If you didn't there are some answers on the next page! Come on...

Just in case there were some you didn't get, here are the answers. And, if your answer is as good or better than mine, I don't mind.

1 Draw a hot air balloon.
2 Draw a a bottle of wine.
3 Draw a roll of film.
4 Draw the sea.
5 Draw a house.
6 Draw a bird.
7 Draw a box of cornflakes.
8 Draw a coconut palm tree.
9 Draw a pig.
10 Draw a book.
11 Draw a skeleton.
12 Draw a map of Italy.
13 Draw a bull.
14 Draw the letter 'B'.
15 Draw a dog.
16 Draw a carton of yoghurt.
17 Draw a washing-up liquid bottle.
18 Draw a jumbo jet.
19 Draw an apple tree.
20 Draw a snowcapped mountain.
21 Draw a sheep.
22 Draw an oil well.
23 Draw a beehive.
24 Draw an ant hill.
25 Draw a loaf of bread.
26 Draw a skyscraper.
27 Draw a suitcase.
28 Draw traffic lights.
29 Draw a shaky line.
30 Draw a bird on water.

31 Draw a barrel.
32 Draw a pyramid.
33 Draw a pair of smoking boots.
34 Draw cracked ice on river.
35 Draw a huge block of concrete.
36 Draw swamp and bubbles.
37 Draw a mouse.
38 Draw 4 tree stumps.
39 Draw a tiny iceberg.
40 Draw 2 empty dangling trapezes.
41 Draw lumpy snow.
42 Draw a tiny box on table.
43 Draw a beard on Guskitt.
44 Draw Wibley with 2 legs.
45 Draw boxing gloves on Geraldine's hands.
46 Draw wig on Harry's bald patch.
47 Draw a hat on Mr Pye.
48 Draw Shortie's long legs.
49 Draw Ivor's feet and legs.
50 Draw ragged edge of painting in frame.
51 Draw rope on ground from window.
52 Draw a rock with 3 spots.
53 Draw a cloud.
54 Draw 2 lots of 3 dots (nose and eyes).
55 Draw rain falling.
56 Draw a snake with 2 lumps.
57 Draw a snapping rope.
58 Draw a water splash.
59 Draw one hippo's eyes.